Dear Sam,

With thanks for being

a wonderful

chapel project, 2010-2011

- much appreciated!

All good wishes

Anthony Buckley

At the harbour side

Considering Christianity

Anthony Buckley

authorHOUSE®

AuthorHouse™ UK Ltd.
500 Avebury Boulevard
Central Milton Keynes, MK9 2BE
www.authorhouse.co.uk
Phone: 08001974150

First published by AuthorHouse 3/16/2010
ISBN: 978-1-4490-6447-1 (sc)

With gratitude to fellow travellers in Ealing, Hereford, Oxford, Folkestone and Dulwich. Particular thanks to my family, Monica, Frances and Richard, to students at Alleyn's school, to Bishop Michael Turnbull and to Amanda Bowring. Their reactions, insights and suggestions were extremely helpful. I bear full responsibility for all the mistakes that remain; there would have been many more without their input.

At the harbour side

Imagine…

You are standing by a harbour and you are wondering whether to take a journey.

Or, perhaps, you know you are already on a journey but you are wondering about the next stage. You think you may have been invited to board a particular boat, bobbing in the water beneath you. There are steps to go down, the gangplank is lowered and you are free to walk across. You are aware that you will not be captain and you are not quite sure where the wind will blow.

You may have considered this boat before. Perhaps you have heard stories from others who have previously set sail; occasionally you may have wondered if you should have a closer look. Or perhaps this has all come out of the blue, and you are surprised to find yourself leaning over the railings, trying to catch sight of what is happening on deck. Perhaps you have been brought to the harbour-side by an event of great personal significance. Perhaps it has been a steady, deliberate, path to this point.

Whatever brings you to the harbour side, you are here. And would like to know more.
What is life like on board? What do I need to be considering? Is the boat really there or is it a trick of the light on the waves?

This short book is an attempt to help people consider what it means to get on board the Christian 'boat'. If the boat imagery works for you, enjoy it. If it does not, ignore it. It is the content, not the wrapping, which matters.

Contents

Chapter 1
What holds this boat together?

Love…

The boy sat next to me at the children's meeting. "What do you want for Christmas?" The speaker asked the audience. People called back with all sorts of answers, mostly electronic and well advertised. My friend looked at his shoes and simply said: "Love." His family was going through a difficult time; he knew that this was the one thing, more than all the gadgets or money on offer, that really counted. The key word in Christianity is the word that speaks most deeply to our needs.

We start with love. The core belief of Christianity is this: God loves us and values us. He enjoys our company and wants a relationship with us. He constantly seeks to renew and restore this relationship. The love of God is not one-way, we are to be caught up in it: responding, sharing and receiving.

In John's gospel in the Bible we are told that God so *loved* the world that Jesus was given. The night before he died Jesus reminded his disciples that their *love* was to be the defining feature of their lives; before that he had told them that all the great commandments can be summed up in *love* for God, neighbour and self. In case the early church forgot this, the leaders kept emphasising the importance of love in their letters.

We might be tempted to think that it would be easier if the key characteristic was something else. Targets such as religious observances, leading a good life, not doing too much harm (or, at least, not being caught too often), are attractive and straightforward. We could work down the list; we could tick the boxes. Love is much more complex. It means that the journey is going to be personal and it will be about relationships: God-wards and neighbour-wards. Our vulnerabilities may be exposed; we may have to face up to what we really are.

But of course love is liberating as well as threatening. Here lies depth and growth, and here is something anyone can receive and anyone can give. A child can love as richly as a king. You do not have to be bright or strong, rich or articulate, to love.

But what is love? It is not the same as indulgence; a parent who allows a child to eat whatever they want whenever they want is not acting out of love. It is not the same as a constant flow of warm feelings; a friend will visit a needy person because it is the right thing to do, whatever the feelings might be. It is not the same as paternalism; love is to be received as well as given. Perhaps it could be said that "Love is relentlessly wanting the best for the person", whether that person is ourselves, someone else, or God himself. What holds this boat together? What is at the heart of this journey? The belief that God loves us and wants the best for us. Utterly.

Questions

Do you agree that love is the right place to start?
What does it mean to you to be truly loved?
"Love is relentlessly wanting the best for the person" –
Do you agree?

...And Prayer

We are surrounded by many models of so-called love and it can be difficult to know what real love looks like. Christians believe that true love is based in the heart of God, modelled in the life of Christ. We thus need to be in contact with him, and so we need to pray.

You may be thinking that it is too soon in a booklet such as this to begin talking about prayer. But Christianity makes unavoidable claims about being a supernatural religion, about there being a God. It talks about relationship more than it does about upholding a set of values. Thus the concept of prayer is important for the serious enquirer. Without prayer it is believed that we do not stay in touch with the source of all we need, without prayer we cannot be open to having a relationship with the captain. Prayer holds the crew and captain together in one team.

Perhaps the word 'prayer' makes us uneasy...

Perhaps we think it is a religious thing to do and we are not sure we are religious.
Perhaps we don't think it works.
Perhaps we don't know where to start.

Briefly on these three issues:

We do not have to be 'religious', or to be in a church building or use particular words, to pray. Heading into a crisis, who does not ask something or someone "out there" for help? In the middle of a wonderful experience, who does not feel thankful? When regretting a wrong action or word, who does not want to say sorry deep down and hope there is a possibility of forgiveness? Who does not enjoy chatting or thinking through the ordinary events of the day? Prayer is as natural as a child speaking to an adult who cares.

But what about when prayers are answered 'no'? We follow in significant footsteps when we feel this happens. Before he was arrested Jesus asked if there was not some other way of carrying out his mission, but it was not to be. He had already entrusted himself to the will of God and did not fight against this answer. Prayer is not a supermarket ("I'll have some of that today, Lord"). Prayer is a committing to relationship with God wherever it might lead, sharing our requests, fears or thanksgivings, but above all trusting we will be resourced for the journey even (perhaps especially) when it is not the path we want or choose. If we sometimes think prayer does not work, perhaps it is because we are expecting it to do the wrong thing.

Where to start? Any words will do, but it is helpful to have a structure and Jesus himself has given us a golden pattern in what, with a small addition at the end, is now known as "The Lord's Prayer" (explored below). Some people use prayers that others have written, some use a pattern such as T.S.P. - Thanks, Sorry, Please. Some people listen to music, go for walks, write or draw as they pray. Some simply speak or think what is on their heart.

God wants us to pray; the relationship matters. If there are moments when we do not feel like it, moments when we realise we have not prayed for days or years and feel guilty about knocking on that door again, or moments when we pretend we are too busy, it is good to bring to mind that God wants us to pray. Remember, this all about love. He likes our company.

Brief extension… The Lord's Prayer

Throughout the Bible and church history there are thousands of other prayers recorded for our encouragement; all that are truly valuable pick up an emphasis that can be seen in the Lord's Prayer.

Our Father in heaven,
hallowed be your name.
Your Kingdom come,
your will be done,
on earth as in heaven
Give us today our daily bread.
Forgive us our sins,
as we forgive those who sin against us.
Lead us not into temptation,
but deliver us from evil.
For the kingdom, the power and the glory are yours.

Now and for ever. Amen

Here is a brief interpretation:

We note that the first word is "Our", not "My". Whenever we pray we are united with the vast host of people round the world and through history who pray to God. We never pray alone even if physically we appear to do so. We are not on a solo journey. The prayer goes on to remind us of the perfect paternal love of God (For those who have difficult memories or images of fatherhood, we can think in terms of "a thousand times better than the best parent we can imagine") but that he exists outside of our limited world. This is no tribal god of a wood or a sea; this is the one God who is in Heaven.

We are reminded that we are praying to a holy God, different from the created world. His love and purposes are pure and just. Perhaps also implied is the thought that God can be honoured through our daily business, through right actions and attitude. In the same way that a head teacher is honoured by good behaviour of pupils, so God's name is honoured through our lifestyle.

We pray for the kingdom, the acceptance of God's authority, to continue to grow, for evil and confusion to be pushed back step by step from apparent positions of strength. We look for, and are excited by, green shoots of love and faith, wherever we may see them. The kingdom grows as our obedience grows. As part of this, may God's will be done in our lives.

It is daily bread we need, not a monthly stock of caviar.

Enough resources - emotional, spiritual, physical, intellectual - to face the challenges and opportunities of today. We are never promised a pain-free life or a safe life. There will be storms and tears, but we can ask for enough to see us through the day. Tomorrow there will be other worries and different weather. We will need to pray similar words again.

We are to be forgiven and forgiving people. Because this is so difficult (at least for most of us) we need God's help, so we pray for this. If we do not think we need forgiving, we put ourselves outside the healer's reach. If we do not want to forgive others we are closing our minds to the forgiveness we ourselves need. The theme of forgiveness is central to Christianity, and will be explored later.

There is much discussion as to what Jesus actually meant by "Lead us not into temptation" (or: "to the time of trial)". To take one, slightly simplistic approach, it is wise for an alcoholic to pray that the off-license will be shut, for the besotted man to pray that that girl won't be at the party. It is wise to pray that the difficulties we face will not throw us off course. There will be dangers on the way, not always immediately recognisable for what they truly are; we need to pray to be kept safe from them.

We finish the prayer by acknowledging that the power and glory is God's, not ours. He can see us safely through.

Questions

What do you think is easy and difficult about praying?
What prompts you to pray?
What hinders you from praying?

Chapter 2
Who is the captain?

Some experienced travellers would say that we should have started with captaincy. Who is running this ship? Who is going to see us safely through? Christianity is unashamedly a supernatural religion. The captain is not a set of values or list of self-help techniques; the captain is Jesus.

To talk about Christianity without focusing on Jesus is like playing football with no ball. We may run around, we may wear the outfit, we may know our positions and practise our moves. It may be a good spectacle, but without the ball it is worth nothing. Christians believe that God has revealed himself in a unique way in Jesus and that he is the way for us to come into a relationship with God.

If we are to start with Jesus, where to begin? It is clear that something extraordinary happened in a small part of the Roman Empire in about 30 AD. This was to shake and transform that empire and then affect the whole world. It was never claimed to be a revolution, a scientific discovery or a war; it was all about a person.

The claims made for Jesus have not been made for anyone else in history. If they are to be explored, then our minds may need to recalibrate to be open-minded enough to see all the evidence. There will be a little more on this in a later section when we explore some of the evidence for faith, for the present we will note what his contemporaries and near-contemporaries recorded.

They noted that he emphasised the inward qualities as much as the outward ones. He commented scathingly on those who want status for its own sake and who love being the centre of attention. He said direct and uncomfortable things about materialism and about giving to the poor. He stressed accountability and integrity.

We are told that Jesus spoke with particular authority. He gave the impression that "This is how it is, whether you like it or not" and sees himself as playing a central role. He is the author who has walked on to the stage; he knows the direction that the play is taking. It is he who will ultimately call people to account. It is he who can lead us to full relationship with God and to rich, deep eternal life – "life in all its fullness".

The most shocking part of his teaching and actions was that they pointed to him in some manner being God. He can forgive sins. He has the power of the creator over illness and death, he is able to still the stormy waters, to feed five thousand people and turn water into wine. He is outside linear time, coming out with statements such as: "Before Abraham was born, I am". He claimed to offer spiritual nourishment that will last forever.

The reaction was as you would expect: hardly anyone quite fully believed it, some people were deeply offended, and some were scared.

He was kind to people that were isolated, mocked, and not in the main stream. He spoke words of comfort, truth and welcome to the marginalised in that society, to tax collectors, traitors, the sick, children, women, the thief on the cross, even a centurion in the occupying Roman army. He was happy to talk openly in the market place or to receive nervous inquirers quietly and privately.

He was a striking figure. There are moments of courage and action (No, you are not going to stone that woman. Yes, I am turning over these tables which you use to cheat people who come to worship. Yes, I will mix with those you call undesirables – and you better look out for your own eternal destiny). It must have been exhilarating and dynamic being with him. People loved him, hated him, were scared of him, worshipped him, wondered about him - but no one ever said he was boring…

If he had been, they would not have bothered to crucify him. Some of the leaders of the province were worried that the watchful Romans would punish a new mass-movement. Perhaps also they were unsure of their status (and the status of the cherished magnificent temple) if all these marginalised outsiders were seen as welcome. They knew that his claim to be God was blasphemous. (Occasionally people say that Jesus did not claim to be God. Those who question this need then to ask why the religious leaders at the time seemed to have no doubt that this was exactly what he was claiming.)

To be fair, not all the leaders were against him: Joseph of Arimathea, Nicodemus and some influential women were persuaded. The Roman governor Pilate was not sure enough to want to condemn.

But enough were opposed to Jesus to build momentum for him to be crucified, executed as a common criminal. There was nothing glamorous or special about the way he died. It was a favoured form of punishment because it was public, humiliating, incredibly painful and 100% successful.

The Sunday following the crucifixion Friday is the transforming moment. The tomb was empty and Jesus was talking to people. A new chapter, a new beginning. He was physical but also somehow more than physical. He ate fish but appeared in locked rooms. The marks of the crucifixion were still there, but he was not battered and broken. He was sometimes easily recognisable and sometimes not. It was not that he had come back *from* the dead, it was as if he had come *though* death. He was himself, but there was a difference.

It is not surprising they took time to believe it, but they could not get round the evidence in front of their eyes. The reaction was summed up in formerly-sceptical Thomas' acknowledgement: "My Lord and my God".

If there really is life after death, as hinted and glimpsed in faiths throughout human history and experience, then our perspective on priorities in this life may need to change. If Jesus was God then the resurrection, this coming through death, was inevitable because death cannot hold God. If Jesus is stronger that death, then he really can forgive sins and offer eternal life. If the resurrection happened then all his extraordinary claims and actions take on a new richness. It is unsurprising that, on this boat, the focus is on the captain.

Brief extension… I have heard rumours – are there three captains or one?

From Jesus' teaching and actions, the early church came to believe that Jesus is one person in the three-person trinity that is God. "The Trinity" is the name given to the belief that God is a relationship of three – Father, Son and Holy Spirit. Jesus told his followers to baptise new members of the Christian family in the name (not names) of the Father, Son and Holy Spirit. It is difficult enough trying to articulate what really happens within the relationships in a family, even more so when describing the three-in-one-ness of God. In spite of the difficulty the early church taught that in the very being of God there is community and fellowship. The love of the Father, the love of the Son, the love of the Spirit. One God.

Questions

Did anything strike you about this brief description of Jesus?
Should some points have been emphasised more and some less?
What would it have been like to be with Jesus?

Chapter 3
Will I be welcome?

The boat is full of people who are there for different reasons. For some there may have been a direct captain-to-onlooker message saying "Come on board". For some, the message will have come through the lifestyle and character of one of the current crew. It is likely that it will not so much be the words that they said, although these are important, but the character that they showed. The crew always welcomes new members. It is not an exclusive club and if ever it appears to be, then it is not getting it right.

You may feel that you are clutching baggage that is going to be out of place when you are on the boat. If you are carrying the burden of always thinking you are right or always should be in charge, of wanting money or status before all else, of abusing sex so it is not about commitment – whatever your burden might be, you will need to be honest about these things: "I want to get on board but as I learn to be part of the crew please help me get rid of these things which keep distracting and slowing me down." We do not get it all sorted in one go; the captain tends to teach and change us at the speed that works for us, not by formula. But our underlying attitude needs to be a desire to be rid of the things that spoil our relationships, well-being and potential. This is what Christians call 'repentance' – a change of heart about our treasured sins.

Since the time of Jesus a sign of welcome to this boat has been baptism. We are physical people and it is unsurprising that we can be helped by physical acts, or that God can use them as vibrant visual aids - and more - to help us. Baptism is known as a 'sacrament', an outward act with inward meaning. Communion is another sacrament, which we will reach in due course. Some branches of the church name other sacraments, but in this short study we will focus on these two.

The washing of baptism symbolises new beginnings and cleansing. It is the sign of welcome into the family of God. It is as if the first thing that happens to us when we climb on board is that we are given a bath, not only good in itself but as a sign of ongoing washing, refreshing and growing that will take place on the journey. Churches differ as to the appropriate age of the candidates but agree on its importance. They also agree that while God is somehow especially at work when someone is baptised, the person themselves needs to live out their baptism, seeing themselves as a fully welcomed and participating member of the crew.

The welcome on the boat should feel a little like coming home. God wants us to feel secure, he wants us to know we are safe, whatever the storms; he wants us to know that food is on the table, that the resources are there. (Think of the homeliness of "Give us this day our daily bread" and indeed of the bread and wine in a Communion service). He wants us to know we are held in love. Coming home has long been an image of spiritual life, summed up in St. Augustine's prayer "Our hearts are restless until they find their home in you". In one of Jesus' stories the metaphor for the errant offspring's renewing journey is coming home.

But, as it is a true home, it is a place where business will be done. It is a place of growth and maturing. Guidance will be offered and behaviour may be challenged. There may be times when we will say: "Do I really want to change? I have got used to my habits and foibles, I know I am not perfect but I have made things comfortable for me and I know how things are". God, the best parent and the best teacher, has more ambitious plans for us. We are not only on a journey, we are also being changed as we travel.

And we need to be nourished for the journey.

Questions

What does "Home" mean to you?
What does Baptism mean to you?
What makes a community of people a welcoming one?

Chapter 4
Is the food good?

Communion

On the night before he died Jesus changed the familiar Jewish Passover words used when taking bread and wine, remembering escape from slavery in Egypt many years before, and applied them to himself. In effect he said: "I am the great liberator from the slavery of sin and death, all previous liberation moments have foreshadowed me." He said that the broken bread and wine outpoured expressed his sacrifice to be made the next day. This was also a victory meal, pointing towards the feast and joy of restored relationship with God. We are to take the bread and wine in memory of Jesus. In some way that we cannot possibly hope to understand, they express Jesus himself.

What is going on? Jesus especially present in the faith of his people as they receive bread and wine? A wonderful memorial? Jesus particularly present in the bread and wine themselves? It is too deep and rich to be fully understood; we are simply invited to take and eat. Christians throughout history have told the Jesus story and taken bread and wine in obedience to Jesus' command to do so. Love given and nourishment offered.

A brief extension...

Baptism and Communion are sacraments for us to receive. Because Jesus commanded them they are seen as very important in the Christian church. Not surprisingly their importance has led people to think carefully about them, sometimes disagreeing (and even, sadly and unnecessarily, then allowing these disagreements to lead to divisions). When children are given wonderful gifts the proper response is a humble and grateful acceptance. We are unlikely to understand how the gift truly 'works'; a brash or insecure friend may pretend that they are the ones who really know why the train can go round the track, but they may be wrong, and the train set can be enjoyed and valued by all present, whether or not we completely understand electricity. We are simply to take and receive.

Questions

Why do you think Communion is such an important ceremony for many people?

A book in their hands

A great deal of what has been written so far has referenced the Bible. What sort of book is this and what is it for?

It is not a long manuscript dictated by angels. It is a collection of books written by people, with all the complexities of human emotion on display, which Christians believe is particularly inspired by God. This collection does not tell the whole story of the universe, past, present and future. The scriptures ("the writings") have a specific purpose; they are to tell the part of the salvation story that we need to know.

Sometimes people ask: Is it literally true? We need to be careful with questions like this. If we were to say "James loves Matilda to bits" the meaning may be true: affection is strong. The imagery, well, is imagery; Matilda is not lying in pieces round the house. The Bible is full of different kinds of literature: History, lectures, letters, story, poetry, visions. Sometimes different kinds are mixed in the same book. When Jesus tells one of his parables we are jumping between history and story in the same chapter. Sometimes there is no explicit indication that this jump is being made, but we sense that this is happening. It is fascinating to read parts of the Bible and to try and work out what sort of literature it is, but the important point is that Christians claim that it all contains inspired, authoritative, truth. The captain may choose to share his wisdom by telling a story, singing a song, writing a letter. "Is this poetry or is this prose?" is a less important question than: "What is God wanting to say to me through this passage?" The means are less important than the meaning.

We may also soberly note that through history and indeed in our own times, people have given their lives so that words from the Bible can be read in people's own languages. Our translations were made at a price.

When we read or listen to a Bible passage it may be helpful to remember the pattern "P.T.P."

We are to be:

Prayerful – that God would say something through it to us.

Thoughtful – What is going on in this passage? It may be helpful to imagine what it would have felt to hear these words in their original context.

Purposeful - What can I learn from this about God, myself or my relationships?

There are numerous patterns of readings, commentaries and notes to help us. When reading narrative, longer sections work well; in other parts simply a verse or two will be enough. It is the quality, not the quantity, of our reading, that matters.

A very inadequate overview of the Bible might include this summary: The Old Testament reveals some key characteristics of God – especially that he is one, creative, holy, just and loving. God's dealings with the people of Israel show what is expected of a community living and growing together and of his passion for them and indeed for the whole world. Through the Old Testament there is a recurring theme that a saviour figure is going to appear; the story is as yet incomplete.

The New Testament tells the story of the arrival of this saviour figure, named Jesus, of what happened to him and what happened next to his followers (the early church). A recurring theme in the New Testament, and foreshadowed in the Old, is that this Jesus will one day return, bringing endings and new beginnings.

Where to start? If you are new to this, Mark's gospel is a good opening. The first four books of the New Testament, Matthew, Mark, Luke and John, are known as "Gospels" because they tell the story, in slightly different ways, of the "Good News" (translation of "Gospel") of Jesus. If you want a selection of shorter passages which cover a variety of themes, you may wish to use the list of passages listed below, roughly enough for a month.

Christians believe that the *acted* word of sharing bread and wine of communion and the *written* word in the Bible both point to the *living* word, Jesus. He wants to resource us for the journey.

Brief extension... Suggested Bible readings

Three Bible writers' sense of purpose
2 Timothy 3:16
   (*2 Timothy* is the name of the book; *3* is the chapter number; *16* is the verse number)
Luke 1:1-4
John 20:31

Two Old Testament writers' perception of God and faith
Psalm 23:1-6
Habakkuk 3:17,18

Events and teachings from the life of Jesus
Luke 15:11-32
Luke 5:17-26
Matthew 5:1-49
Matthew 6:1-34
Matthew 7:1-29
Mark 4:35-41
John 3:16
John 10:10
Mark 10:13-16
Matthew 28:16-20
John 6:35
John 6:68
John 8:57-59
Luke 19:1-10
John 1:1-14
Matthew 11:28-30

The early church begins to work out what being followers
of Jesus means
 Acts 2:42-47
1 Corinthians 12:12-22
1 Corinthians 13:1-13
1 Corinthians 15:1-14
1 Peter 2:23-25
Romans 8:1-17
Romans 8:18-39
Philippians 4:1-13
1 John 1:8,9
1 Corinthians 13:1-13
Galatians 5:22-26

Questions

Does the idea of reading the Bible seem easy or difficult?
If you are going to begin reading, where will you start?
If you are used to reading the Bible, which passages would
you add to the above list?

Chapter 5
What else do I need to know about my fellow-travellers?

A speaker once said:

'When Jesus returned to heaven after his time on earth the angels asked: "What happens now with your wonderful plan for renewing humanity and indeed the whole world, for ushering in a new kingdom of love and justice?" Jesus replied that he was leaving things in the hands of a few followers in and around Jerusalem. One angel looked at the motley collection of confused and uncertain men and women, whose track record of understanding and courage was not, to be honest, all that great. He gulped and paused, and then nervously asked: "Excuse me Lord, and what's plan B?"

"There's no plan B" Jesus replied.'

And there wasn't, and there did not need to be. For those ordinary people were renewed by the Holy Spirit, the third person of the Trinity. The church was born.

As he was preparing to complete his earthly ministry

Jesus promised that the Holy Spirit of God would guide and strengthen his followers. The Spirit is not physical; he is not limited to one place as Jesus was during his time on earth. Jesus could not be in Jerusalem at the same time as he was in Bethlehem. The Spirit can. This needs to be, literally, a "Spirited" crew, a crew knowing they need the captain's Inspiration.

It is a spirited crew and a gifted one. The early church learned that God-given gifts are offered for the benefit and encouragement of all. This is not like being on a cruise ship where, if you wish, you can go the whole journey locked in your own cabin and pretending the other passengers do not exist. In fact there are no "passengers" on this ship at all. Everyone is crew, everyone is in the team. We must play our part, and help our neighbour play their part. They will have skills and gifts that we do not have. We will have gifts that they do not have and we should not keep them hidden. There are several lists of "gifts" recorded in Paul's letters to the early church; some may seem exotic, some may seem ordinary. All are seen as valuable and vital to the well being of the whole.

Spirited, gifted and also a *fruitful* crew. Paul was a key figure in guiding the early church as it tried, in various locations, to work out what it meant to be followers of Jesus. In Galatians 5 he describes the "fruit" of the Spirit as being "love, joy, peace, patience, kindness, goodness, faithfulness, gentleness and self-control." In 1 Corinthians 13 he describes what love looks like: "Love is patient, love is kind. It does not envy, it does not boast, it is not proud. It is not rude, it is not self-seeking, it is not easily angered, it keeps no record of wrongs. Love does not delight in evil but rejoices with the truth. It always protects, always trusts, always hopes, always perseveres. Love never fails"

It may be worth asking if any of these qualities are particularly unfashionable or ignored in the circles we keep. We may be in situations where faithfulness and self-control are mocked. There may be people (perhaps ourselves) who rather enjoy keeping records of wrongs.

There is not space here to comment in detail on each of the qualities but, for example, we may note that:

Gentleness is not easy if we are in a situation where people want obvious displays of power. But in reality true strength is seen in gentleness. Anyone (sadly) has the physical ability to hurt a baby; gentleness comes in using the strength to protect, not to crush. The same can be said of all our relationships, it is vital to learn to hold, not to squeeze. Gentleness is not about being a doormat; it is about knowing that we do not have to throw our weight around.

Patience similarly is a sign of strength and trust. To have the courage to wait, to know that we do not need to force the issue, to know we do not have to get there first. The Spirit can set us free from the fear that causes us to insist on our "rights" now.

The human institution known as the church has got many things wrong over the centuries. This is unsurprising, as it is filled with people like you and me who do not always make good decisions. But it is a matter of historical record that it has also got a large number of things right - think of schools, hospitals and countless offers of comfort and care; think of the millions of people trying quietly to serve their neighbour day by day. These are the times when the institution manages to catch up with the real, spiritual church. These are the times when everyone is playing their part, people are valued for what they are and what they can contribute, people are trying to be faithful in their praying, loving and obedience to the captain.

The early church met together, ate together, learnt together, prayed together. Underlying it all was a profound commitment to each other. Tradition has it that outsiders commented: "See how these Christians love each other". All ages, backgrounds, abilities were there. These are the fellow travellers: very human, but inspired by the captain to be gifted and fruitful. He does not wait for us to be perfect. The roles and tasks are prepared for us, as we are. There are sails to be unfurled, decks to clean, encouragement to be offered, look-outs to be posted.

What do I need to know about my fellow-travellers? They are people, just like us.

Questions

What is most people's impression of "Church"?
What do you think is God's vision for the Church?
What might happen to our attitudes, relationships, our churches and our society if the "fruit" of the Spirit were more evident?

Chapter 6
But I feel a bit rubbish…

"I am not going to fit in. If I get on board I will make the boat dirty, be a nuisance, and spoil things for everyone else."

The great news is that Christians know that they are not perfect. (If you think you are perfect, this is not the boat for you.) Jesus stressed that he could only really do business with those who knew they were in need, who did not get everything right and who knew that sometimes, to be honest, they were not as pleasant as they would like to be. Forgiveness is always on offer and this boat's crew knows that they need it.

A summary of Jesus' message might be: "I know what you are like, I know what you have done, and I would love to have you on board. In fact I would do anything, have done everything, to welcome you here."

Sometimes, sadly, people think they are too sinful or broken to get on the boat. Through no fault of theirs (but sometimes it is the fault of the church) this is seeing things exactly the wrong way round. We are needy people. That's why we are here.

Question

How do we get the right balance between knowing we are not perfect and knowing we are profoundly valuable?

Chapter 7
…But I do want to play by the right rules

We get it wrong, but something deep in us wants to get it right; that's why it hurts when we feel a bit rubbish. Part of love is that we want to play by the right rules and to hear the right guidance so that we don't hurt others. If we are going to be on the boat, we want to be a help, not a hindrance.

The athlete was overjoyed – he had reached the finishing line first. Raising his arms in a celebration of victory he noticed that there seemed to be little applause. He looked around him and saw an official approach him. "The egg has to stay on the spoon," the man whispered.

Part of our deep desire to get it right may mean re-thinking how we should be running the race. The athlete in the egg and spoon race had been using the wrong criteria. Our society bombards us with images about success and failure: get appearance, status or money right and you will finish the race in triumph. But what if these criteria are the wrong ones? We may think we are crossing the line to win but what if we were running the race with the wrong rules? Some in the crowd may applaud, but perhaps they have got the rules wrong, too?

In the eyes of Christ, if today is to be a successful day, then we will be living it with love, compassion, honesty and justice. It is not so much what we do, it is how we do it. We may make a large sum of money or be told we look amazing, but if we are not doing this in love then we have deeply failed. Conversely, we may make all sorts of mistakes and sometimes look stupid, but if we have managed to try to show a little love and faith on the way, then it has been a gold medal day.

Martin Luther-King said simply, in a sermon on Mark 10:35 in February 1968 that was then replayed at his funeral, "Everybody can be great because everybody can serve."

Some of us can put up with nearly anything except the feeling that we have made a wrong decision. Perhaps it did not make us as happy or as rich or as famous as we thought. Perhaps it was part of a grand strategy that now seems to be unravelling. Perhaps we always prided ourselves on our discernment and wisdom, and now our friends are shaking their heads and believe we have lost our way.

But we may not have done so. It seems that in the eyes of God the 'how' we decide is as important as the 'what'. If we choose to do something thoughtfully, prayerfully and lovingly, then it is the right decision. If we are manipulative or selfish in the decision-making, it is the wrong decision.

On board the boat we will begin to realise that the captain is as interested in our thoughts as in our behaviour. Members of the crew are called to attend to their inner selves, not at the expense of outward actions, but rather that these actions can be properly shaped and resourced. Paul urges his readers in the early church in Philippi to fill their minds with good things. "Whatever is true, whatever is noble, whatever is right, whatever is pure, whatever is lovely, whatever is admirable—if anything is excellent or praiseworthy—think about such things."

This list is well worth using as a reference point as to what we watch, listen to and think about. (Perhaps newspaper editors, television producers and computer programmers should have it on the walls of their offices.) If we are going to *do* good we need to *think* good.

Questions

What are the criteria for success and failure that we use in our lives?
Where did we find them?
What values would you like to be shown in your life?

Brief extension… The Ten Commandments

Jesus said that the greatest commandments were to love God and love others as we love ourselves. He said that these summed up the commands given in the Old Testament. The most famous of these were the Ten Commandments (There was a time when nearly every church building had a copy of the Ten Commandments inscribed on the wall).

These words were given to the Jewish people as they were being formed into a community and a nation. In our society where there seems to be an uncertainty about the validity of any kind of rules at all, it is helpful to see the themes underlying the words. Here is an abbreviated version, with short reflections. We may see links to the Lord's Prayer and to what is called Jesus' "Sermon on the Mount", recorded in Matthew 5-7.

A community begins to be formed (Exodus 20:1-17).

"I am the Lord your God, who brought you out of Egypt, out of the land of slavery. You shall have no other gods before me."

There is one God. One source for good guidance as to how we live our lives. There are not thousands of tribal deities inhabiting woods or hills, each one being equally valid and offering equally valid guidance. There is one God, listen to him. He is the God who is part of our story and he is the God who rescues.

"You shall not make for yourself an idol in the form of anything in heaven above or on the earth beneath or in the waters below. You shall not bow down to them or worship them."

We are not to worship an image, or put all our resources into chasing anything man-made (or man-imagined). An idol will not deliver what we need and it distracts our attention from God.

"You shall not misuse the name of the Lord your God"

We are to see God's name honoured ("name" is tied closely to identity.) We should be careful about our choice of words. On a deeper level we should be very careful about doing things in the name of God if we are using that phrase as a cover for our own motives and agenda, not his. It is all too easy to manipulate others through religion.

"Remember the Sabbath day by keeping it holy. Six days you shall labour and do all your work, but the seventh day is a Sabbath to the Lord your God. On it you shall not do any work, neither you, nor your son or daughter, nor your manservant or maidservant, nor your animals, nor the alien within your gates."

We are to live a balanced life, especially ensuring there is a balance between work and rest. We note that the command to keep the Sabbath includes a command to help other people keep it. Workaholics not only harm themselves, they are also deeply unhelpful role models for others.

"Honour your father and your mother, so that you may live long in the land the Lord your God is giving you."

We are to honour our parents; this means that we realise that society has a structure; security and stability demand that we work within it. For those with difficult or absent parents, we can widen the applications to the parental figures in our lives. We need to make the most of the wisdom and experience of the older generations; it is a win-win result if they know that they are honoured and valued.

"You shall not murder."

We do not have the freedom to take someone's life just because we feel like it. It sounds obvious, but think of the difference to our streets if everyone obeyed this, and we knew they obeyed it. There is also the implication that power is always to be guided by morality.

"You shall not commit adultery."

I was once with a class of non-religious teenagers who, unprompted, wondered if adultery should be illegal. They had seen the damage it had done to their families. Self-discipline, faithfulness, commitment and honesty are all caught up in this, as is the obvious issue of sexual self-control.

"You shall not steal."

We are not to steal people's possessions or anything they hold dear - their dignity or their hopes, for example.

"You shall not give false testimony against your neighbour."

We are not to lie about other people. Whether it is in court or in casual conversation, we should not manipulate words to cast another person in a bad light.

"You shall not covet your neighbour's house...or anything that belongs to your neighbour."

It does not make us happy if we envy and desire someone else's possessions or reputations, and it destroys the relationship we have with them. It shows that we have forgotten that we are loved and valued as we are.

Question

Do you think the 10 Commandments are still relevant today?

Chapter 8
Does the captain ever get cross?

Jesus did not shout at the occupying Romans or the prostitutes, but he did get angry with hypocrites. He was criticising those who indulged in a deliberate misplacing of priorities, focusing on praiseworthy outward actions instead of the bigger and deeper issues of love and attitude. There is a particular emphasis in his teaching (indeed throughout the Bible) on the value of integrity.

Do we deliberately give an impression on the outside that does not match what we are thinking on the inside? Note the word 'deliberate'. Of course we all do things from mixed motives and we want to appear at our best. It becomes a problem when we consistently, deliberately, choose for the outside to be different to the inside. It is dangerous when we wear a different mask so that we burden others, either by condemning them for sins which we are perfectly happy to allow to fester in the hidden places of our own hearts, or by pretending to be what we are not, which can lead to others feeling inadequate.

When Jesus said that we were to be like children perhaps one of the characteristics he was affirming, alongside the key virtues of love, trust and humility, was transparency.

You know where you are with a toddler; what you see is what you get. As we grow up we become very skilful at separating the inside and the outside. The inconsistencies that this creates can be harmful to ourselves and to our relationships. Much of Jesus' teaching was about sorting out what goes on in the inner person, knowing that this then shapes the outside. Too often we are tempted to worry just about how we look on the outside. We do well to remember Jesus' question "What does it count to gain the whole world but to lose your soul?"

We should note that, as well as showing frustration with hypocrites, Jesus made it crystal clear that those who sought to harm children were heading for deep trouble. There is a cold and certain anger in his words on this issue. The cries of the vulnerable, whether children or others, will not go unnoticed.

He also got angry with those who put up barriers for others to express their faith in God. Thus the tables at the entrance of the temple were turned over.

The captain is full of love and compassion, but that does not mean that anything goes. Quite the opposite, it is *because* he is full of love and compassion that true justice will be exercised.

Questions

Why is hypocrisy so destructive to real relationships?
How good is our society at looking after the welfare of children, and others who are vulnerable?

Chapter 9
Will I just be lazing around?

Work, responsibility and leadership

There will be tasks to be carried out and work to be done. The boat needs looking after, not only for its own sake but also for all those who encounter it. We are entrusted with responsibility. When we get down to our homework, the report for the boss, the next course of bricks, the kneading of the bread, the saying of prayers, the visiting the lonely, or the cleaning the oven, the work is to be respected. And those who work, we should honour.

We are using the word 'work' in its widest sense. There is no distinction in the Bible between the value of paid and unpaid work; it is all service to be done wholeheartedly in the name of God. There is no such thing as an unimportant task in our service on board ship.

In our society we perhaps especially need to watch that we are not tempted to think that the value of work is measured in terms of the size of the salary. We also should remember that those who manage others have a responsibility to honour the work of employees or volunteers and to ensure it is as interesting and fulfilling as possible. The mundane is valuable for what it achieves, not because it is mundane. There is no intrinsic value in keeping tasks boring in themselves when, with a little thought and care, they could be developed and enhanced. How can a task be shaped and valued so that the person doing it can see most satisfaction in the doing of it?

Martin Luther-King said in December 1956: "Whatever your life's work is, do it well. A man should do his job so well that the living, the dead, and the unborn could do it no better. If it falls your lot to be a street sweeper, sweep streets like Michelangelo painted pictures, like Shakespeare wrote poetry, like Beethoven composed music; sweep streets so well that all the host of heaven and earth will have to pause and say, 'Here lived a great street sweeper who swept his job well'."

Whatever we are called to do on our journey, let's do it well.

Most of us exercise leadership at some stage of our lives. It may be at work or at home; it may involve responsibility for a pet, a large and complex endeavour, a tea trolley or a family.

On this boat the model of leadership centres on service. Jesus washed the feet of his friends the night before he died. The captain does not sit in a luxurious cabin; he got – and gets – his hands dirty in his identifying with the crew.

As we exercise different forms of leadership we can

remember that selfish ambition will not be the driving force of this leadership. We will be willing to hear both sides and to see the whole picture before coming to a conclusion. We will be willing to build good relationships because this is the best way of knowing what is going on in the organisation and because there is a fundamental understanding that people matter.

There will, unsurprisingly, be a focus on integrity. The leader's behaviour needs to match the responsibility given. There will be honesty about mistakes made and a willingness to help others through their mistakes. We are taking responsibility not because we are ruthlessly ambitious or we have fallen into it by accident; we are taking it because we have been asked by the captain to do it. We feel honoured to be entrusted with it.

Part of knowing about leadership is knowing when you are under someone else's authority. At certain times a chief executive is wise to obey a lollipop man. I may be an expert at cleaning the deck but I need your leadership if I am going to help unfurl the sails. The overall purpose will always be more important to good leaders than their own personal status.

Questions

How do you honour work and responsibility?
What good and bad leadership have you experienced?

Chapter 10
Well, I'd like to laze around a little…

Rest and play (a brief return to the 4th Commandment)

Our society can be, for some, quite a driven place. We may need to re-learn the childlike ability to rest, and equally to learn to allow others to rest. We may need to learn that, in the eyes of this particular captain, the aspiration to achieve the right balance between relaxation and work, between the needs of family, friends and our employers, is more important than striving only for work-based targets.

For some of us, we may need to relearn the joys of harmless pleasures. Of course the adjective "harmless" is vital. If we are harming ourselves or others then the activity will be destructive. We may have felt that fun and games should have long been put behind us, but there is a childlike humility in doing something simply because we enjoy it. A favourite book or walk, a time with friends. Hot chocolate and Beethoven. If we struggle to think, "What do I enjoy?" then it is too long since we did it.

Sometimes we say or do too much because we want to

control a situation; we are scared of it slipping away and so we throw a net of words or actions all round it, closing off every escape route, pinning down anything that looks loose. On this boat we don't have to talk *too* much. We don't have to do *too* much, either (although occasionally laziness may need to be addressed).

Being quiet and restful means trusting that we don't have to nail everything down. It means we have time to hear the voice of the captain, through others, circumstances, the church, our praying and our reading. Inner quietness is a mark of humility; it is a resting in the love and purposes of God.

It is not the same as opting-out, of being detached from others or from situations. It is not the same as childishly thinking that we are above such things as laughing and chatting with friends. It is part of a Sabbath lifestyle, learning - this can be a shock - that we are *part* of the crew. We are not the captain, entire ship's company and owner of the ship rolled into one.

Being over-busy can even be a semi-deliberate ploy to shut off the voice of the captain; perhaps this is why it is such an insistent theme in the Bible that we take time to be still, and to listen.

When the disciples rush to wake up Jesus during a storm on the Sea of Galilee we read in Mark's account that he was resting his head on a cushion. We may think of heroes as stoical and pain-free, who think nothing of laying their head on a bare wooden deck. There may be times when this is appropriate, but we hear that in this case

Jesus used a cushion. Perhaps it was already on the boat, perhaps he had brought it with him, perhaps someone brought it for him. Wherever the cushion came from, it was not spurned: a little bit of comfort was not seen as a bad thing.

One final thought – is it better to multi-task or to do one task well? If we are emailing while eating while watching TV while responding to a text while chatting to someone in the room, then do we need to ask how well we are handling all the relationships involved?

Questions

How do you honour rest and leisure in your life?

Chapter 11
Will it be an easy ride?

We need to be well resourced (welcomed, nourished, praying, loved and loving) because it is not going to be plain sailing. There are no promises that the journey will be smooth. We get on this boat because we think it is the right boat, not because we think it will provide an easy ride. It may be 'home' but there are times when the weather is bad or we do not understand what is happening, or both.

What might be the difficult times? How might we face them?

Tempted

We have noted that there are high expectations for attitudes and behaviour on this boat, but we have also noted that we are to be honest and aware of our shortcomings.

Sometimes we get it wrong; we let down the crew, the captain and ourselves. If we think this is a problem then we will want to be prepared for whatever may trip us up. Inevitably, temptation is a personal area – what tempts me may have no hold on you, and vice versa - but there

45

may be some general thoughts worth considering. Underlying temptation to sin is the temptation to think that God has got it wrong, that he does not have our best interests at heart and that we know a much better way to achieve the satisfaction we crave. It is somewhat unlikely that we do…

Or perhaps we think that *this* time he will not notice.

Temptations promise so much but deliver so little. This is why some are addictive: we look for the next thrill because we hope, against all experience, that *this* time we will achieve what we are really looking for.

Another trick is to get us pre-occupied with thinking we are winning a battle in a small area while the real attack is happening on undefended territory elsewhere. We think we are facing an attack on our determination to avoid eating three doughnuts each day, while in fact this is a feint, the real attack is coming in encouraging us to be increasingly selfish, spiteful or proud and we do not notice. (Or pretend we do not notice).

And so sometimes we fall. We sense the chalice is poisoned but we still choose it. The crucial issue is what we do next. If we persist in holding it to our lips, drinking again and again of the potion, with no regret, then our well-being will suffer, deteriorate and eventually die. If we turn to Christ, honestly admitting that we have made the wrong choice in this particular action, thought or conversation, then he takes the cup from us, cleans us up, and nourishes us with forgiveness and love. In some way beyond our understanding, Jesus' death on the cross is especially significant in soaking up our sin. He took it all on him, experiencing the separation from God, from all that is good, that sin causes.

The captain knows where we need to be going; he understands that sometimes, strangely, we scrabble out over the side of his ship to reach another craft that momentarily is glinting in the sun. If we turn our face back to the ship he will launch the lifeboats and welcome us back, bedraggled and covered in seaweed as we might be. Always.

C. S. Lewis wrote to a friend in January 1942: "I know all about the despair of overcoming chronic temptations. It is not serious, provided self-offended petulance, annoyance at breaking records, impatience etc. don't get the upper hand. *No amount* of falls will really undo us if we keep picking ourselves up each time. We shall of course be very muddy and tattered children by the time we reach home. But the bathrooms are all ready, the towels put out, and the clean clothes in the airing cupboard. The only fatal thing is to lose one's temper and give it up. It is when we notice the dirt that God is most present in us: it is the very sign of his presence."

Brief extension…

Temptation can indeed be an issue for those on the boat; but when we think of it we should equally consider forgiveness and mercy. In ourselves and for others we can be dismayed by sin, but not by the sinner. We can speak firmly against a bad act but we are not to crush the person. We are to be gentle people, inwards and outwards. If we can see that God longs to forgive us for what needs to be forgiven, and that this is a free gift, then we will inevitably want to be forgiving and merciful people. This is not the same as pretending that no-one sins against us. It means facing up to the fact of the wrong done, acknowledging it and then saying that the relationship is bigger than the sin. We may be wounded enough that we need space from the person for a season, but we still value them and want the best for them.

Part of being merciful (and just plain sensible) is to realise that there is a difference between a mistake and a sin; they need to be responded to in different ways.

Part of being merciful is being generous with our gifts, our time and our money. It is sad when we are mean-spirited rather than Holy-Spirited. Jesus said a great deal about not being trapped by the worship of money and similarly on the need to show charity to the poor. Our giving should be an expression of a free and giving nature, of a response to the divine generosity that we ourselves have received.

Tired and flat

Sometimes we will be tired. Or the boat may seem to be in the doldrums and all is flat. In 1 Kings 19 in the Bible we read that the prophet Elijah had won a great victory against the prophets of Baal. The people of Israel had witnessed the power of God and the long-awaited rain had arrived. But instead of a warm-glow of satisfaction of a job well-done Elijah felt very flat: "I have had enough Lord".

Sometimes, unexpectedly, we can feel low. Everyone else might be thinking that all is going wonderfully well and we do not have a care in the world, but inwardly we are saying: "I have had enough".

The Bible is very honest about our tendency to get fed up. (The psalms are full of such anguish.) In the Elijah narrative, we are given an example of what can be done to help.

First, Elijah was allowed to sleep and eat, sleep and eat. As simple as that. His body was restored to normal rhythms.

Second, he was given a purpose. It is disheartening to feel we have no purpose. It is a continual biblical theme that God has purposes for his people. There is always something valuable that we can do (sometimes simply by "being").

Third, he was told he was not alone. Hard on the heels of feeling purposeless is feeling that we are the only one. It is good to remember that we are part of a big crew.

Through this narrative we can be encouraged by the truth that when we feel flat we are not the first to have done so. And, of course, if we feel that this "flatness" may be symptomatic of medical depression, then it is entirely right to seek advice. There is a strong Christian tradition of affirming and encouraging medical expertise.

Doubting and questioning

We are whole people. Our minds like to be stretched and our feelings can fluctuate. This is unsettling, even though it again follows the pattern of many people in Christian history. Later we will explore some of the evidence that can support faith, but with all the evidence in the world there will still be fog banks, when nothing seems clear or conclusive. Two brief thoughts at present -

First, if it is a question about our feelings changing then perhaps it is helpful to remember that God sometimes takes away feelings of peace and assurance because he does not want us to rely on the feelings in themselves. Comforting feelings are happy reminders, but the underlying Christian belief is that we are profoundly loved whether we feel it or not. We can see why these withdrawal moments may be important – my feelings can be all over the place depending on weather, conversations or even the performance of the England cricket team. If my faith is for real, it needs to be rather more foundational than that. Thus when the feelings change, it may be less pleasant but it may not be a bad thing; it can help us to look to the core of what we believe and why we believe it.

Second, we will sometimes have specific questions. If so, whom can I ask or what can I read to help with these? We are unlikely to be the first to ask such things and it is wise to ask what previous or fellow travellers have to say. If our heart is to be exercised by loving then it is entirely appropriate for our minds to be exercised by questioning.

But there may be frustration. It is not easy to hold the balance between rigorous intellectual searching and the realisation that there will be some explanations beyond our grasp. If God is for real then some things will be beyond our understanding. The alternative is a person-sized and thus person-invented religion.

Sometimes on the journey we will not understand what is going on in the boat, or why it is going in a particular direction. That is not quite the same as wondering if the boat truly exists, or even necessarily that it is the wrong boat. We may sometimes want to ask significant questions about the actions of our employers. We may not understand them or may disagree with them, but we still believe that they exist.

Doubts and questions may be healthy but they can be disturbing, challenging and frustrating. However, it is not a sign that things are going wrong; the opposite can be true if we end up being led into a deeper understanding.

Taking an unpopular stance – justice matters

Another difficult part of the journey may be this. It is not enough to be nice (although that is difficult enough); we are called to be people of justice and this may mean being unpopular. We should be putting right those things that are unfair. We are to protect the vulnerable; perhaps a colleague who is always being put down or ignored, perhaps people further afield who can be helped through legislation, campaigns or charities. The sea across which we travel is full of situations and adventures that need our involvement. That means that there will be times when we challenge local powers or when we remind them of their responsibilities. Perhaps we are called to exercise authority ourselves; we then have a particular calling to be models of justice.

As ever, we must start locally. Part of treating people fairly is learning to set aside our own ambitions and to understand our own motives. If I am determined to put person B in the shade so I am noticed by person C, then I will manipulate situations and conversations to my advantage. I am not being just. Or, if there is an ongoing feud with person D, I may read the worst into all his words and not give him a fair chance.

These dynamics happen in families (and churches) as much as they do in the work place and schools. An audit of "do I always treat others justly?" would be a challenging exploration for many of us. Even more so would be the question "Do I stand up for justice for others?"

We will not always get many bouquets for taking such a stand.

Learning hard lessons

There may be times when we need to learn something about ourselves. And for a reason beyond our understanding the particular lesson in question has to be taught to us through experiencing a tough situation. We are allowed to sail into some bad weather. This is not saying that the bad weather is specifically, deliberately, caused for this purpose. The existence of suffering, great and small, is much more complex. Perhaps friends disappear, or the job stops going well. Perhaps some security in our life is taken away or we have to face disappointment in our past or in our future expectations. Such times are not easy. Yes, our perseverance and boat-craft are being strengthened but it is still a painful season.

Of course we can equally learn about ourselves during the comfortable times. Whether it is a beautiful day or a storm-filled one, part of our calling is to become more self-aware, more able to be honest and open with ourselves. It is not always easy.

Grief stricken

Sometimes we will be sad. The reality of love means that we share in people's sufferings and we deeply grieve when we lose what is special to us (albeit temporarily – in terms of eternity we will never lose what has been truly good). Jesus himself wept at a funeral. A feature of this boat is that people take suffering seriously, realising that it hurts, that there are no slick responses and seldom an easy way through. The crew does not glorify suffering, still less yearn for it, but honours and supports those who go through it. Grief can be a holy place; it speaks of love for the person and self. It is a place where Jesus himself stood.

It is not a sign of failure to be unhappy when things are sad. This may sound obvious, but there may be tempting voices saying that we always need to look happy. The world is not always a happy place. If it were, there would have been no need for Jesus or the ongoing work of the Spirit; we will sometimes see tears on the face of the captain as well as on our own.

(The Bible verses about being joyful are more to do with inner strength and assurance than having a perpetual smile on our face.)

Sickness, whether emotional, mental or physical, is part of the world we inhabit. Occasionally miracles happen and there are wonderful healings, direct divine foreshadowing of that time when, we are told, all suffering will cease. But, in biblical accounts and now, these are the exceptions. Until all things are renewed and there will indeed be a "new heavens and a new earth", there will be suffering. All possible help and support are to be offered and sought. But the suffering still hurts.

Brief extension...

A very common assurance in the Bible is "Do not be afraid". Fear seems to be such a part of human existence that we frequently need to be reminded that we have been invited to be in the right boat and that we will indeed be seen safely home. Often it is the uncertainty as to how we will handle things that scares us, as much as the event itself. With the captain, we will cope. Perhaps battered and confused, but we will cope.

Questions

How do you face the temptations that particularly affect you?

Do you find it easy to forgive and to be forgiven?

Is it healthy to talk about doubts and questions?

How difficult is it to stand up for justice in your situation?

Occasionally one hears the view "get on board and all your problems will disappear" – how would you respond to that?

Chapter 12
Is the boat really there?

Is there a boat there at all? Perhaps I am just being allured by the sun on the water and the spray in the air? Perhaps I was tempted by a glossy brochure but the company went bankrupt years ago and never had a real boat to advertise?

It may be helpful to remember that there is much in current western culture and thinking that appears to want to tell us that there is no such boat. Those who want to explore belief face more adverse pressure for doing so than at any other time in our history.

We may think that it would be so much easier if we could see or touch God, but in reality it would cause more difficulties. If God were visible and tangible he would be within and part of our physical universe. If God is God, then he needs to be bigger than that. (And of course the Christian narrative says that God did appear on earth in Jesus; at one point in history he was touchable and the reactions were exactly the mix of adoration, fear and uncertainty that we would expect.)

It may be helpful to remember that our important life

choices very seldom rely on physical evidence. We enter a career, friendship or marriage because of numerous intangible pointers.

So what are the pointers for Christianity? Why might this be the right boat? The full list of evidence that has proved useful to people runs into many volumes. Presumably there is already some evidence that you are considering, otherwise you would not have picked up, or been given, this booklet? We are all different: here are eight pointers that have been of help to me. They are not "knock down" arguments – the big decisions in life tend not to work like that – but they have been enough to make me feel that a faith position is a sensible and reasonable one to hold, that there are good enough grounds for thinking that it is very likely that the boat is there.

1) The problem of suffering. Whether or not you believe in God, suffering exists. The fact that it is a problem to us implies that we have a strong sense of justice. We see children suffer in a far-off country and we not only say: "That is so sad" or "I'm glad that is not happening to me." We also say: "This should not be happening". The "should" implies a moral framework where compassion and justice are highly prized. It speaks of our sense, our deep memory, that the world should not be like this; this matches the Christian narrative that humanity is in some way fallen and our world is flawed. The fact that we respond so strongly to suffering does not sit easily with the idea that we are simply a collection of chemicals. We may ask: "If there is a God of love, why is there so much

suffering?" This is a valid and important question, but equally significant is "If there is not a God of love, why does suffering matter so much?"

2) We react powerfully to beauty and to new life. Consider the joy and wonder of seeing the new-born baby. Consider our reaction to sunsets, art, sport or music. When we sense the vastness of the universe we use words such as "awesome". Where do these feelings, this appreciation, come from? Perhaps our response to beauty and to new life speaks of our being made in the image of a creative God.

3) The historicity of Jesus. As noted above, Jesus of Nazareth is unique in world history in what, according to the records, he said and did. There are references in Jewish and Roman literature to Jesus as well as the historical records in the New Testament. The validity of the biblical record is a crucial issue. These records have rightly been challenged, tested and analysed more than any other documents in history but still they hold up. Those who are seriously interested in this area will understand that we cannot do it justice in a few sentences in a booklet such as this and I commend further study.

As always in serious questioning, the key requirement is open-mindedness. If we approach the Battle of Hastings determined to believe that Harold was not shot in the eye with an arrow then we can argue away that particular scene in the Bayeux tapestry. If we study Jesus while refusing in any circumstances to accept the existence of the supernatural then that says more about our initial faith position than it does about our historical open-mindedness. If we study Jesus willing to see where the evidence leads, then it is hard to avoid the conclusion that something extraordinary was happening.

Trying to leave all faith pre-suppositions behind, for and against, it is clear that something deeply significant happened around 30AD in that particular corner of the Roman Empire. All the old dreams and glimpses of a life bigger than the physical are claimed to have been fulfilled in a tangible person in our human story.

4) The vast majority of the human population throughout history has believed in some sort of God. The atheist argues that they all are completely wrong. The agnostic, more humbly, feels there is not enough evidence to agree or disagree with these multitudes. As a Christian I can see truths in many faiths and respect them, honouring our agreements and disagreements, uniting with them in affirming supernatural reality, while still maintaining my belief that truth is most fully found in Christianity. Let us here simply note that there is a spiritual hunger across all cultures and backgrounds. Any other hunger is the response to the existence of the object desired. Physical hunger is met in bread, emotional hunger in relationships. The desire to worship implies that somewhere there is some sort of God.

5) We are all shaped by those whom we meet. I keep coming across people with gentle, persistent faith, still strong and growing whatever they have been

through. Observing their lifestyle and courage I can't help but think that there is some sort of reality here. I note also the presence of faith in the lives of so many significant thinkers and campaigners in history. At the very least, I need to take this seriously. Can such a variety of people – from Alfred the Great to Elizabeth 1st to Martin Luther-King to Mother Teresa to Elvis Presley to J.R.R. Tolkien to child X next door and widow Y down the road - all be *completely* wrong? If I am hesitant to say that they are utterly deluded, then, if my search is genuine, I need to ask how I can find out more about this common factor that they seem to share.

6) There seem to be times when some (perhaps many) people experience something they can only describe as including some sense of the 'other', the spiritual, perhaps God. I could try and explain these moments away but then feel that I am not being true to what people tell me (and indeed to my own small experiences). This is a subjective argument; but religious experiences will always include a subjective element and may be none the less genuine for that.

7) We live in a universe of amazing order, variety and complexity. We are accustomed to think in terms of "laws" of nature. It is possible that the presence of such laws is a pointer to the existence of a creative, ordered, mind.

8) We desire meaning and purpose. We want to know that we matter. If we hear Shakespeare's Macbeth declaim that life "Is a tale told by an idiot, full of sound and fury, signifying nothing" we note that he

has been driven to this despair and that by this point he is not seeing the whole picture. Perhaps it could be argued that it is only wishful thinking to hope for a value beyond being a collection of molecules. But it is significant that this "wishful thinking" itself exists. We want to be more than eating and breeding machines. The very fact that we ask existential questions may mean that existence is bigger than the tangible.

Questions

These "evidences for belief" listed above – Which help you and which do not?

Are there others that you would add?

Do you have specific questions you would like to ask about evidence for God? If so, whom will you ask or what might you read?

There are some who may feel this chapter is unnecessary. They feel their own experience is strong and certain enough. Do you agree?

Chapter 13
You say this is a gift, not a sale?

The invitation is there.

The captain and the crew want to welcome us on board. A word of explanation, even of caution. We have not been invited because we can afford the ticket or because we understand how to sail a boat. We have not been invited because we have any 'rights'. We have not been invited because we are connected to someone already on board or because we have tried to be good for days, months or years. We are invited because we are ourselves. God enjoys our company so much that he wants to spend eternity with us. Likes and loves us so much that Jesus came, at indescribable cost, to restore the relationship that we kept spoiling through our wrong-headedness. Thus we don't throw our weight around on this ship (we have no weight to throw). We have not earned our place; we have been given it. It is magnificently exciting and thrilling. For those of us who like being in control, it is also a little unsettling. It is all about *grace*; it is a gift freely given.

Question

"A gift, not a sale?" - How does this make you feel?

Chapter 14
What next?

This has been a very brief introduction to a profound question: Is this the right boat for the journey? Whether we like it or not, we are all on a journey; we all choose some sort of craft, some structure of reference points, some sort of captain, to trust. We all need to answer the questions: What boat are we on? Why have we chosen it?

This may have been a frustrating and inadequate read. Perhaps there have been times when you have wanted to take points further, times when you have wanted to engage and to argue.

You may feel you want to explore further. Find a wise person who is already on the Christian boat and ask what it is like for them. Or turn back to the suggested Bible readings. Or discuss with friends where you feel the thinking in this booklet is helpful and where it is weak, or what it was that brought you to the harbour side in the first place.

You may feel that you have heard enough, here and elsewhere, and you want to get on board. Take the step of saying a quiet "yes", however tentative or firm, and find a group of fellow-travellers; share in the resources of word, prayer and sacrament. It may be an encouragement to know that millions and millions have stood where you are standing, have got on board, and would say that it has been good. Not always easy, comfortable or straightforward, but still good. Not crystal-clear or doubt-free, but ultimately, deeply, good. The right boat with the right captain.

You may of course already be on the boat and simply wished to read someone else's thoughts. Perhaps you could then consider what you would have said if you had been writing a booklet like this. All our emphases and insights will be slightly different, that is part of the fun of the journey.

Wherever you are on the journey, thank you for taking the time to read this booklet. I wish you well.

Anthony Buckley, 2010

About the Author

Anthony Buckley is a Church of England minister, writer and speaker who has served in schools and parishes for twenty years. Much of his time is spent with individuals or with larger groups, exploring what faith might mean for people today. This short book came out of these discussions.

Lightning Source UK Ltd.
Milton Keynes UK
11 July 2010
156828UK00001B/17/P